CoLoRiNG BooK
ANAToMY
and physiology
FoR KiDS

KEEP
KIDS
BUSY

THIS BOOK
BELONGS TO:

_____

_____

_____

Each image is printed single-sided to prevent bleed-through.

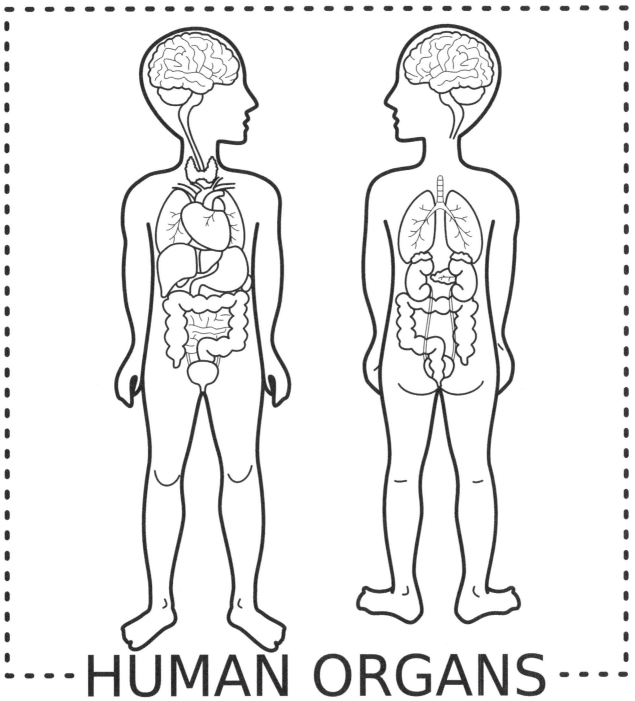

HUMAN ORGANS

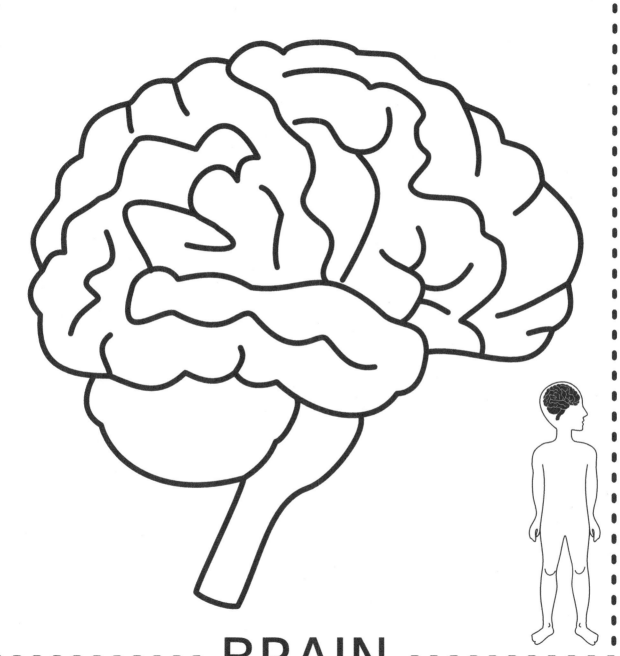

BRAIN

Each image is printed single-sided to prevent bleed-through.

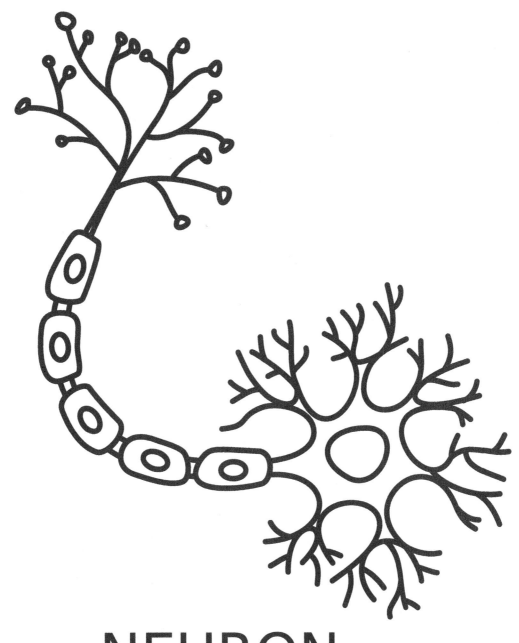

NEURON

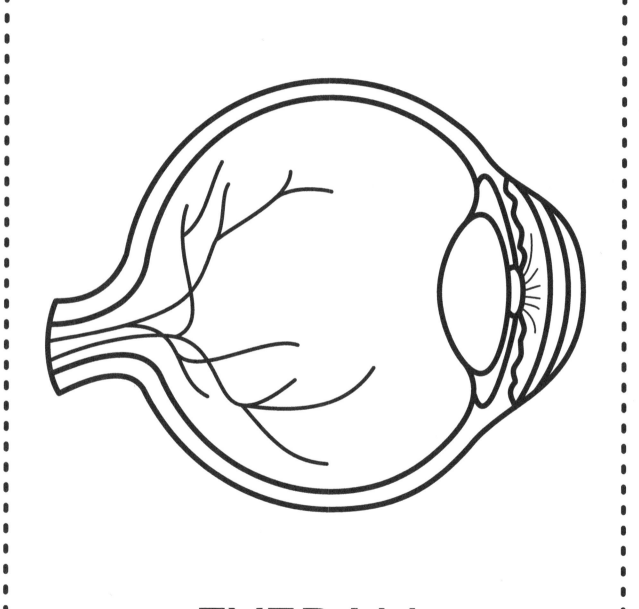

EYEBALL

Each image is printed single-sided to prevent bleed-through.

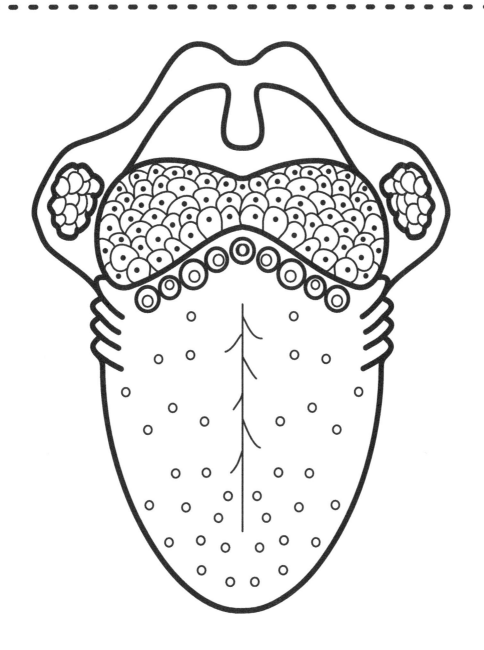

TONGUE

Each image is printed single-sided to prevent bleed-through.

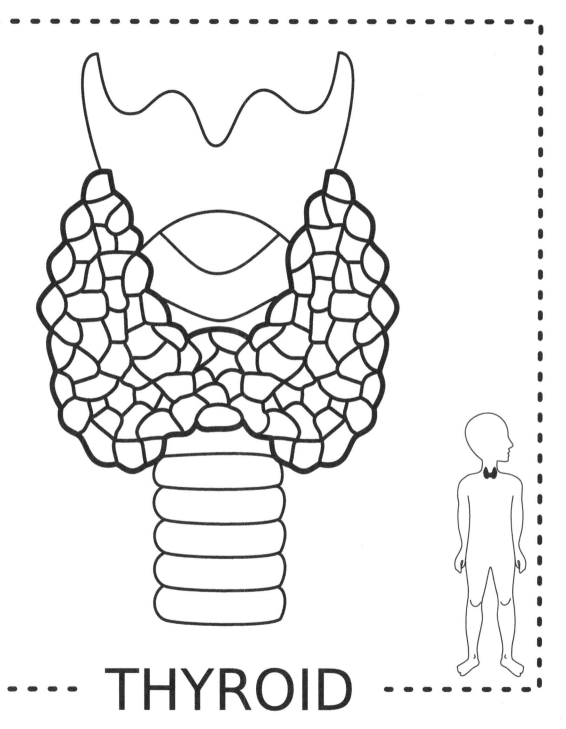

THYROID

Each image is printed single-sided to prevent bleed-through.

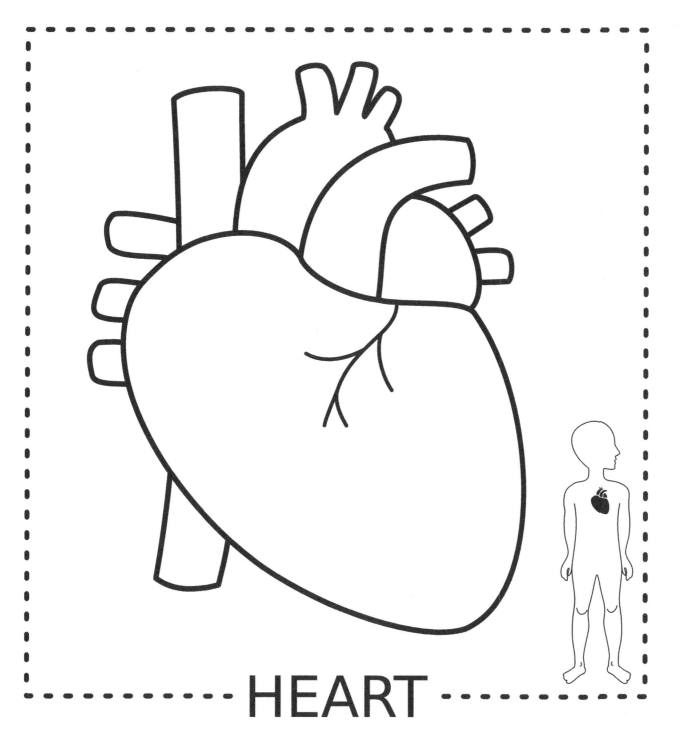

HEART

Each image is printed single-sided to prevent bleed-through.

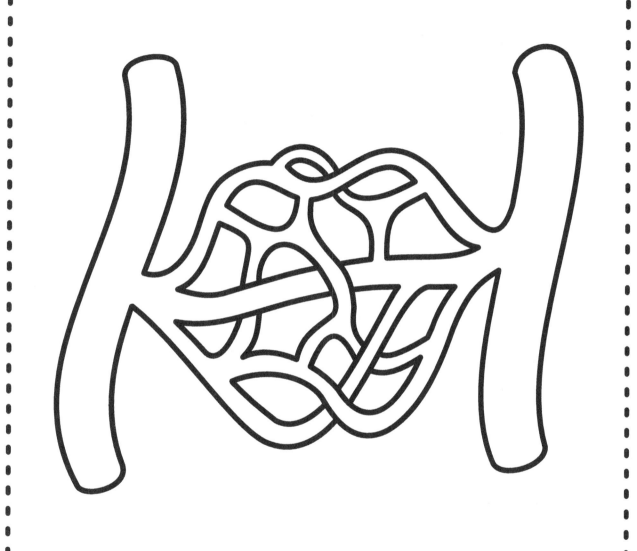

BLOOD VESSELS

Each image is printed single-sided to prevent bleed-through.

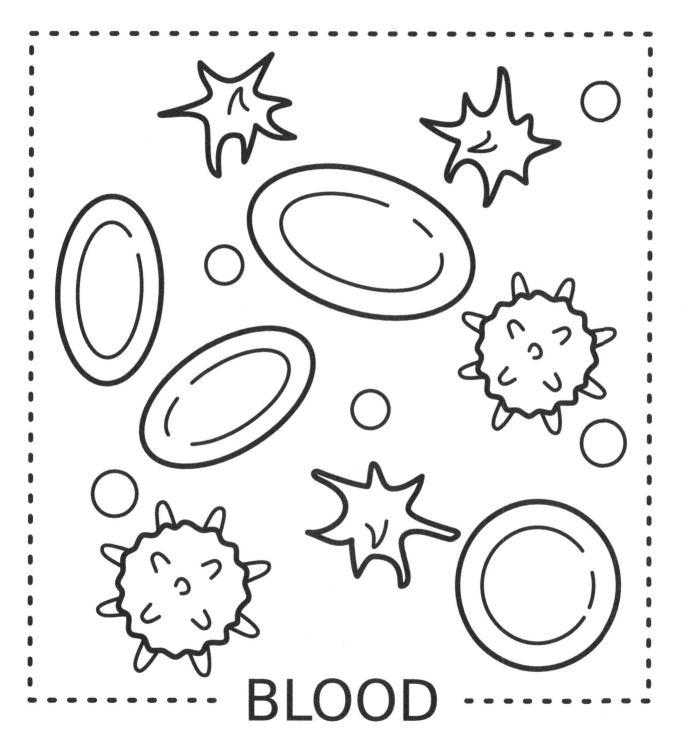

BLOOD

Each image is printed single-sided to prevent bleed-through.

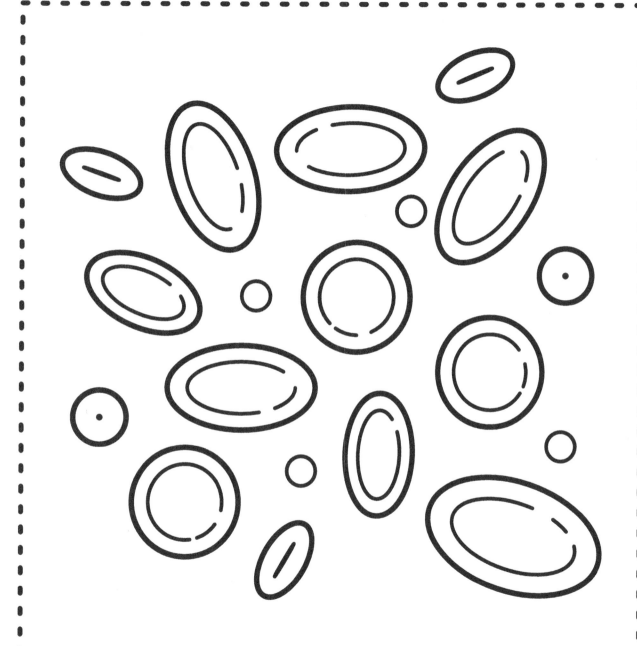

RED BLOOD CELLS

Each image is printed single-sided to prevent bleed-through.

WHITE BLOOD CELLS

Each image is printed single-sided to prevent bleed-through.

PLATELETS

Each image is printed single-sided to prevent bleed-through.

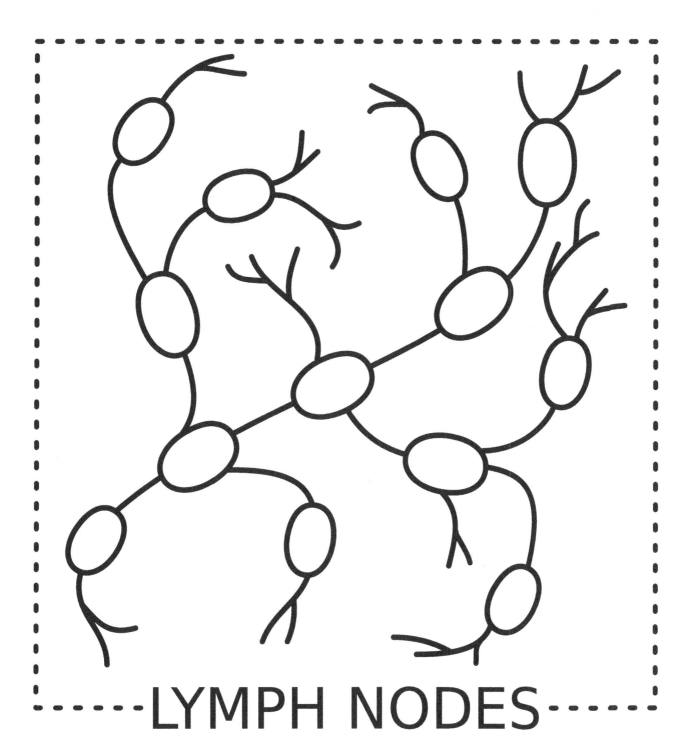

LYMPH NODES

Each image is printed single-sided to prevent bleed-through.

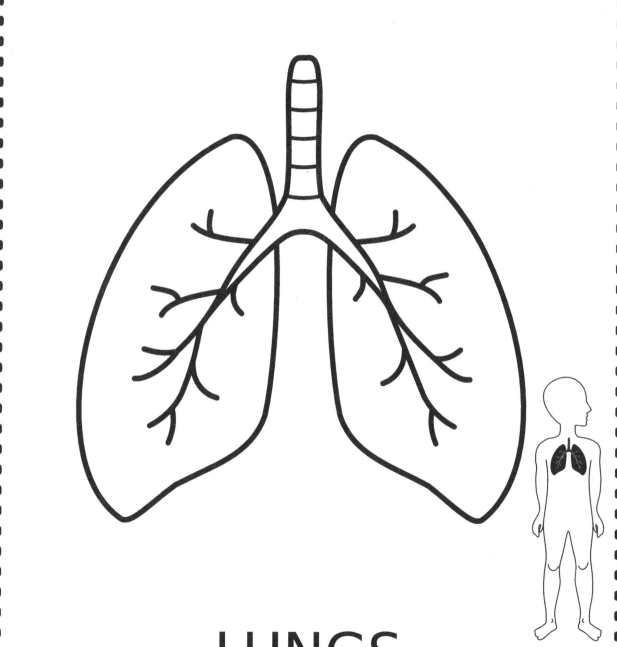

LUNGS

Each image is printed single-sided to prevent bleed-through.

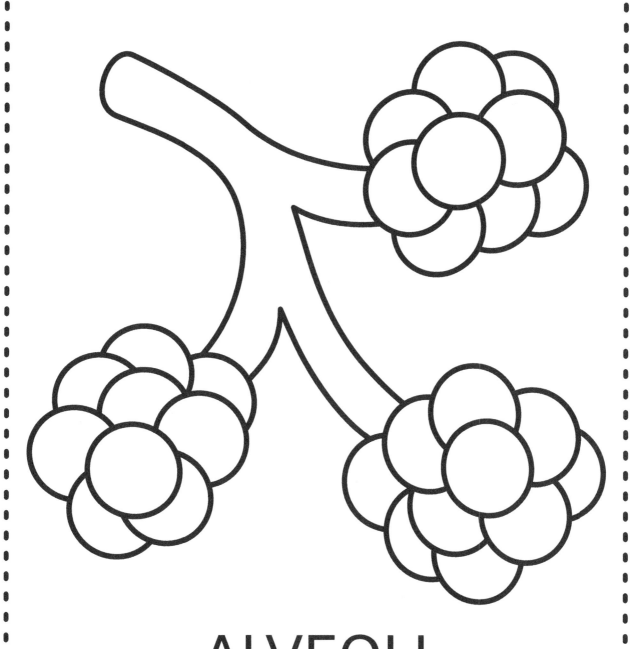

ALVEOLI

Each image is printed single-sided to prevent bleed-through.

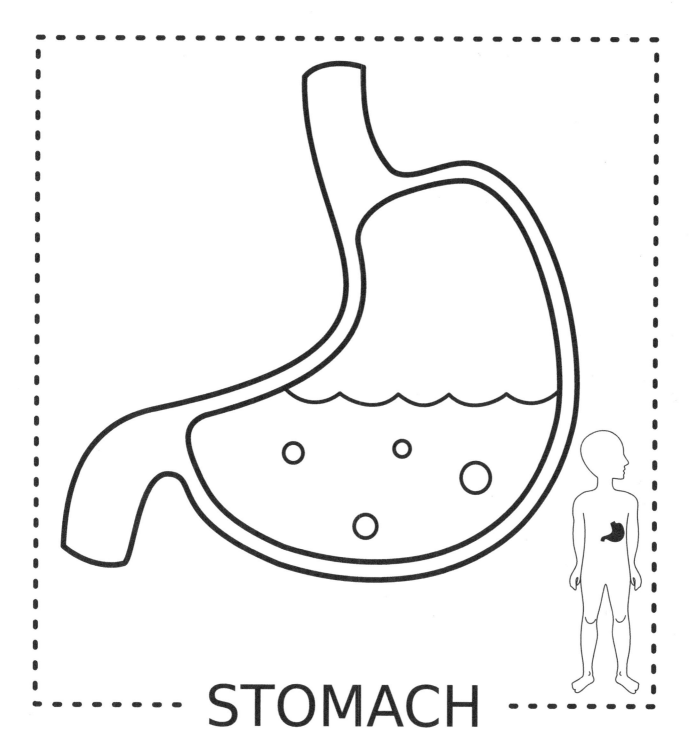

STOMACH

Each image is printed single-sided to prevent bleed-through.

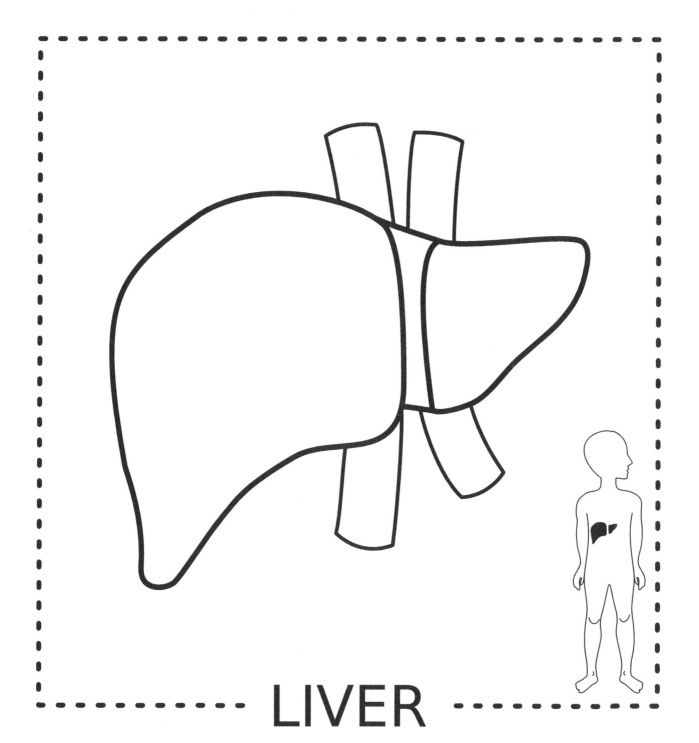

LIVER

Each image is printed single-sided to prevent bleed-through.

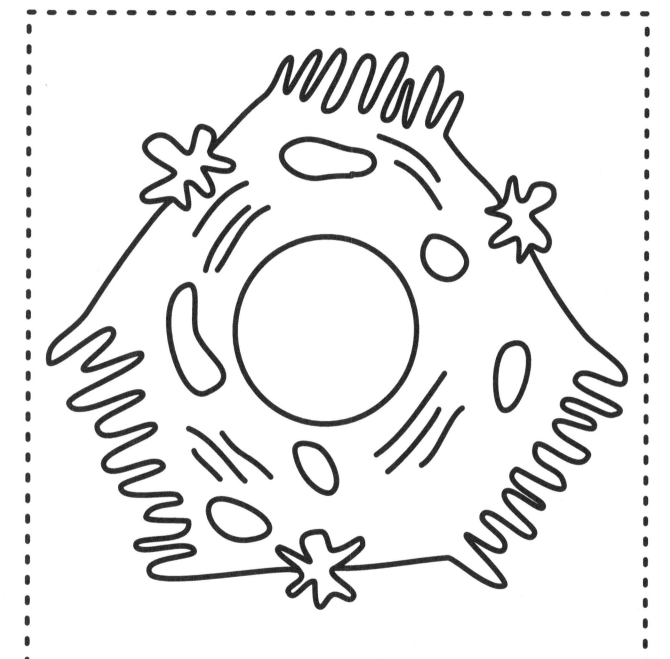

LIVER CELL

Each image is printed single-sided to prevent bleed-through.

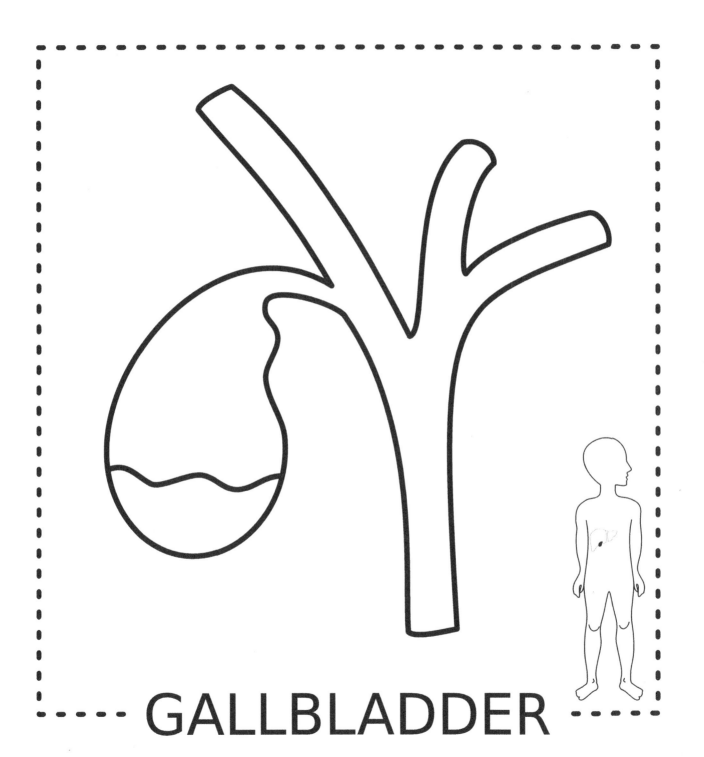

GALLBLADDER

Each image is printed single-sided to prevent bleed-through.

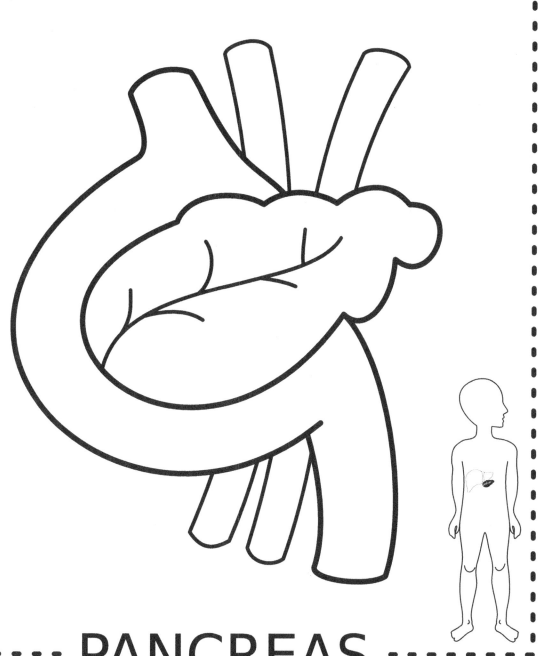

PANCREAS

Each image is printed single-sided to prevent bleed-through.

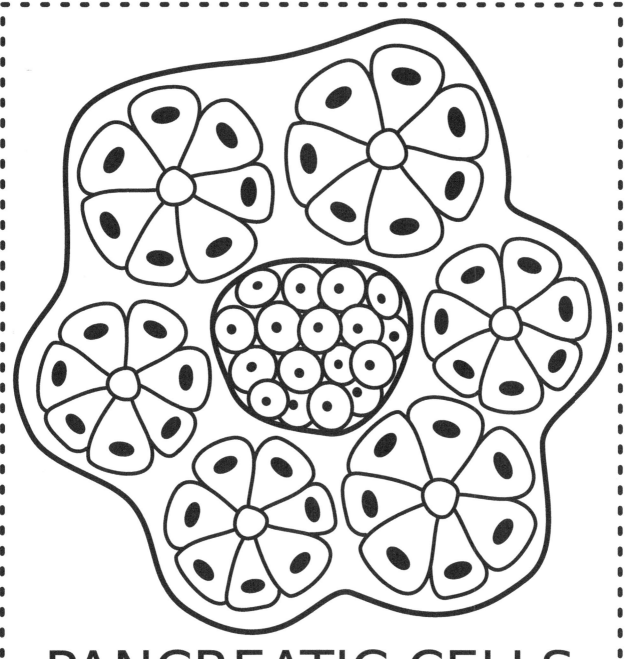

PANCREATIC CELLS

Each image is printed single-sided to prevent bleed-through.

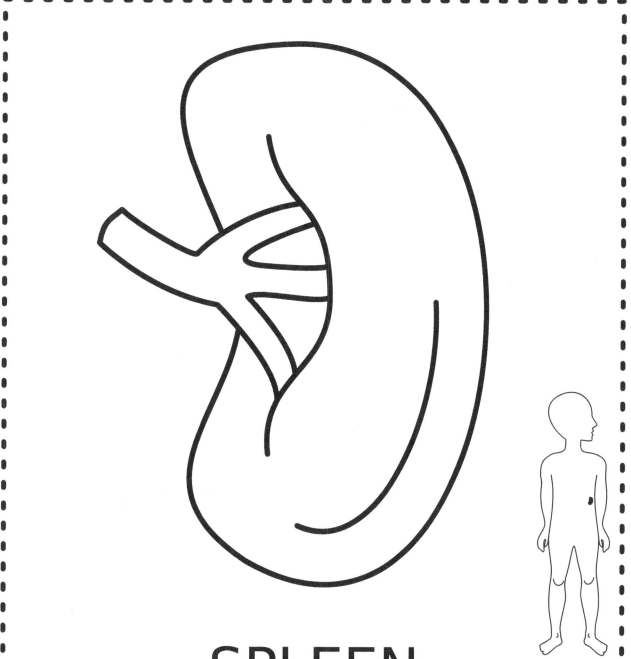

SPLEEN

Each image is printed single-sided to prevent bleed-through.

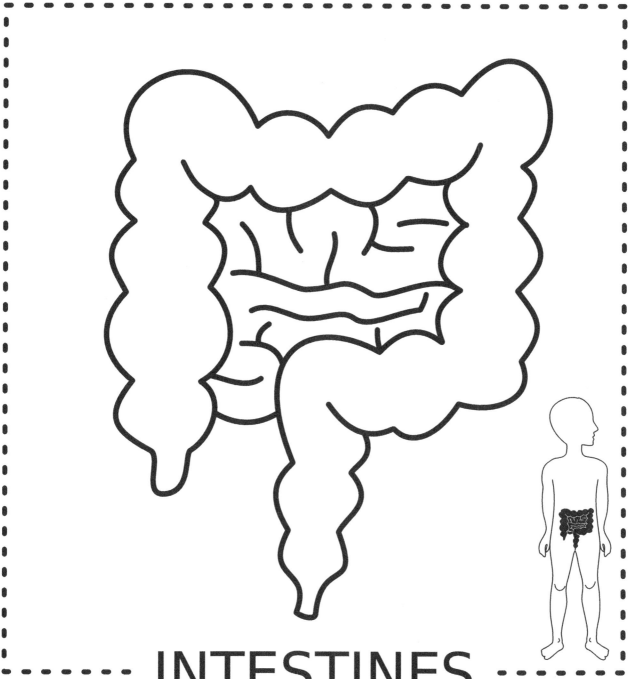

INTESTINES

Each image is printed single-sided to prevent bleed-through.

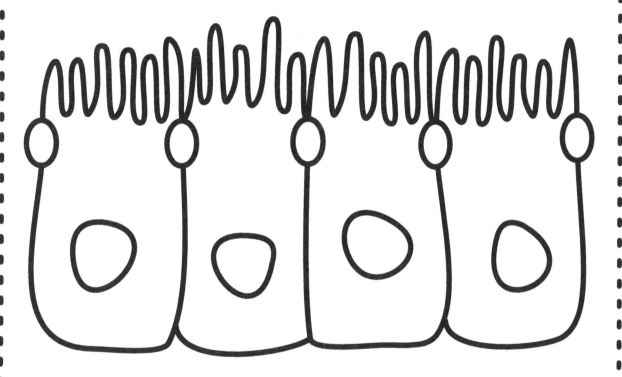

INTESTINAL CELLS

Each image is printed single-sided to prevent bleed-through.

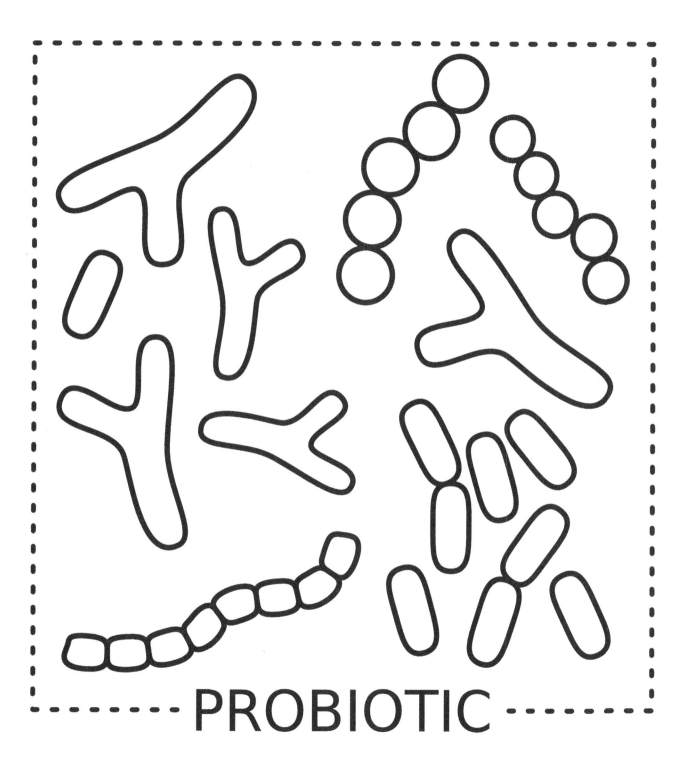
PROBIOTIC

Each image is printed single-sided to prevent bleed-through.

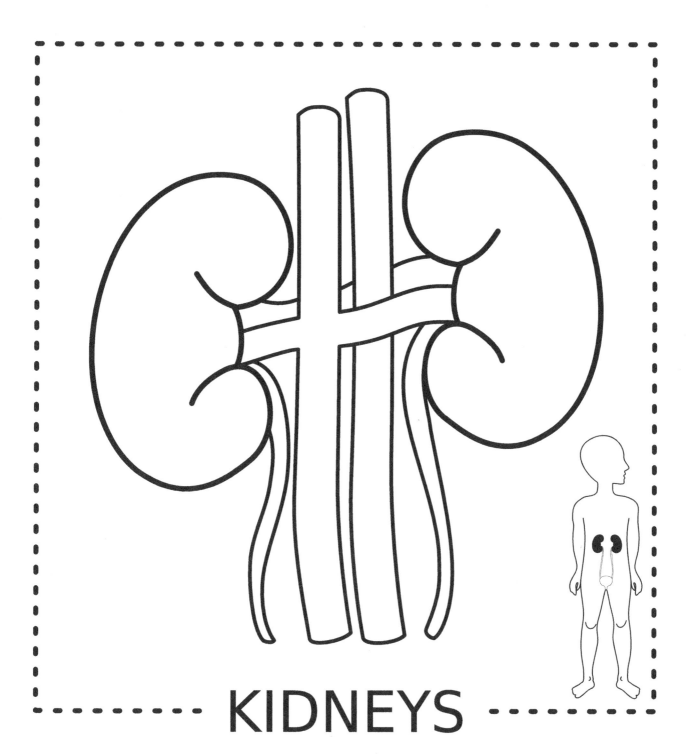

KIDNEYS

Each image is printed single-sided to prevent bleed-through.

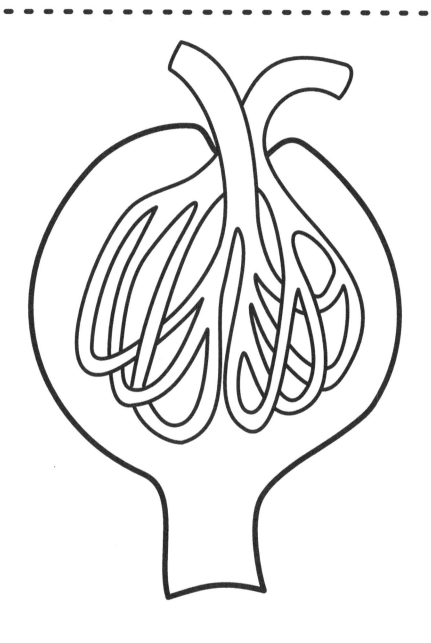

GLOMERULUS

Each image is printed single-sided to prevent bleed-through.

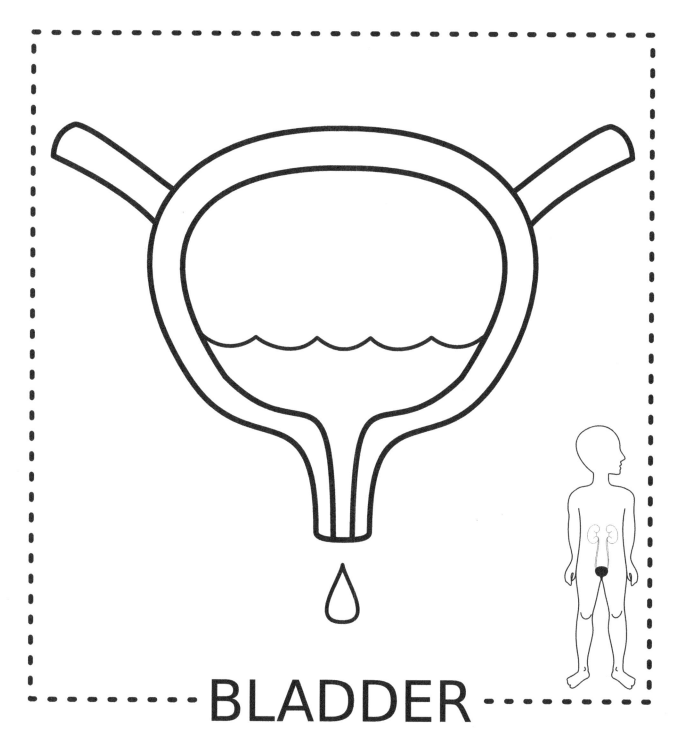

BLADDER

Each image is printed single-sided to prevent bleed-through.

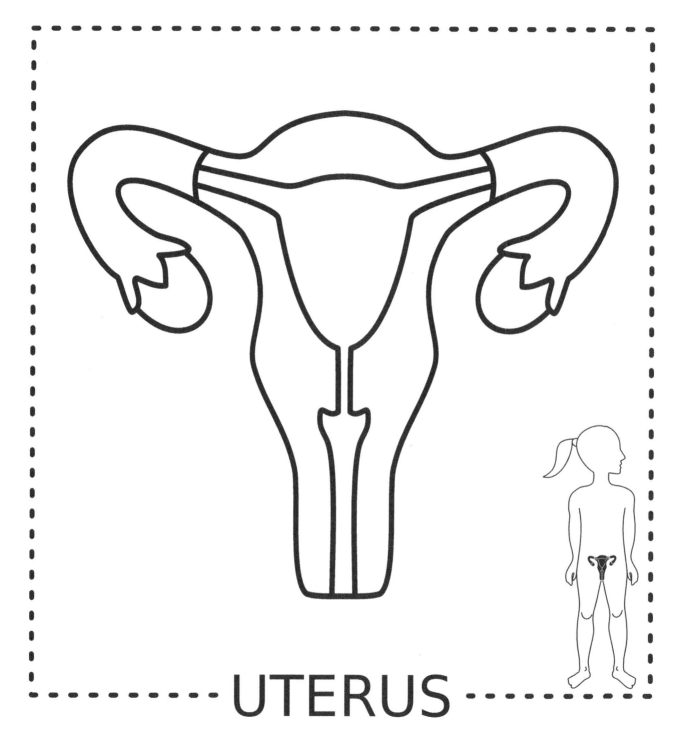

UTERUS

Each image is printed single-sided to prevent bleed-through.

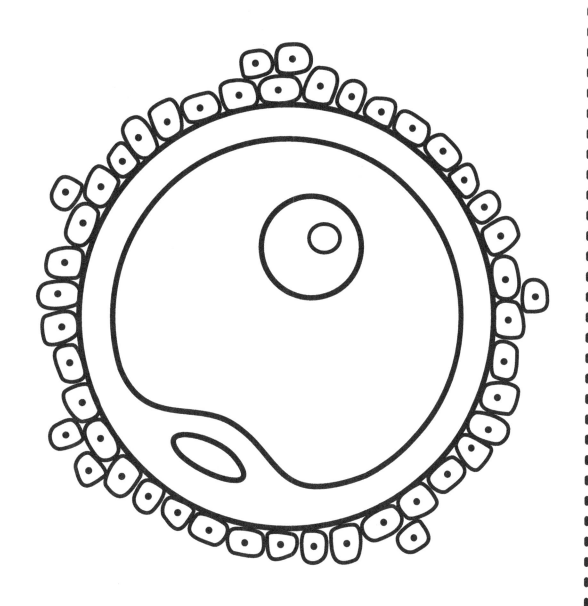

EGG CELL

Each image is printed single-sided to prevent bleed-through.

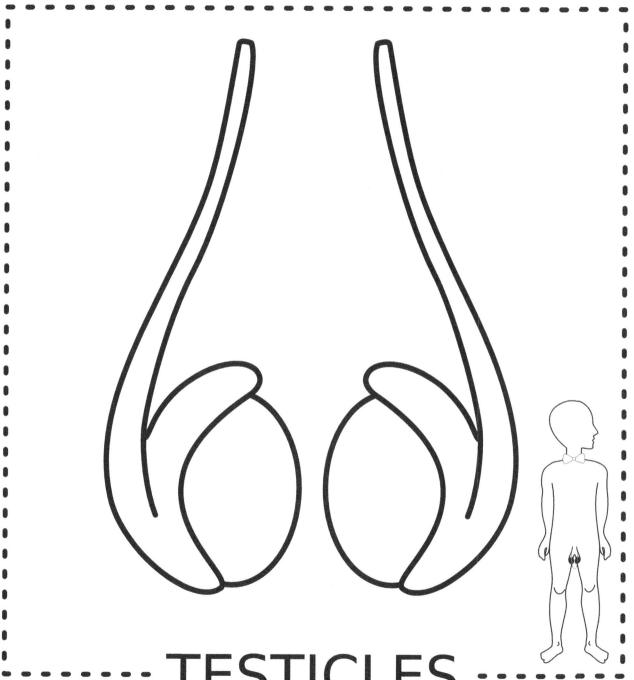

TESTICLES

Each image is printed single-sided to prevent bleed-through.

SPERM CELL

Each image is printed single-sided to prevent bleed-through.

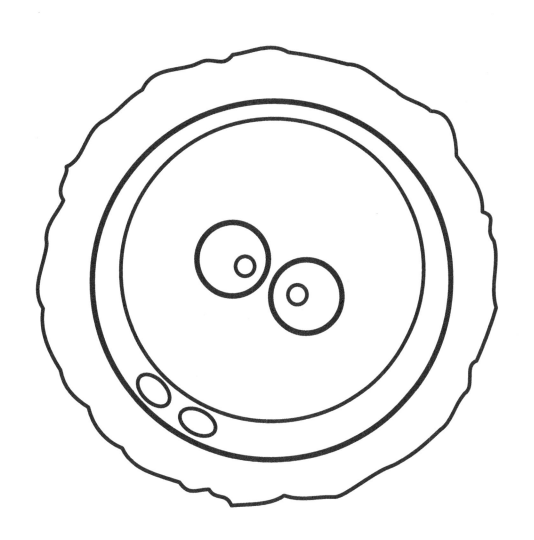

ZYGOTE

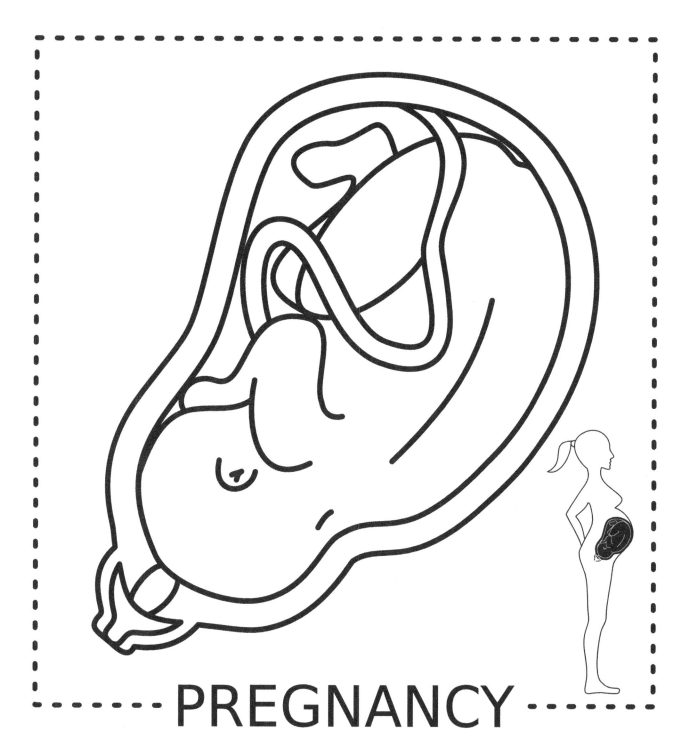

PREGNANCY

Each image is printed single-sided to prevent bleed-through.

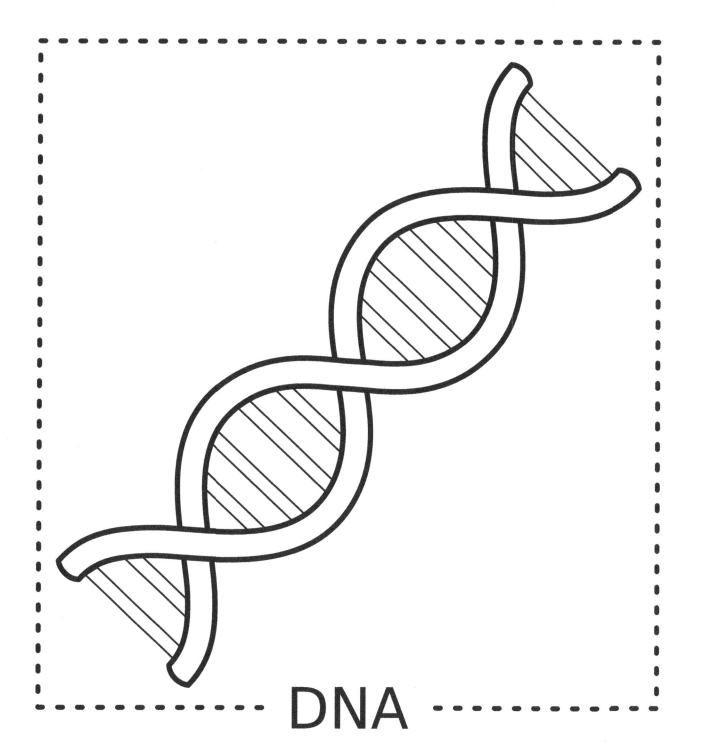

DNA

Each image is printed single-sided to prevent bleed-through.

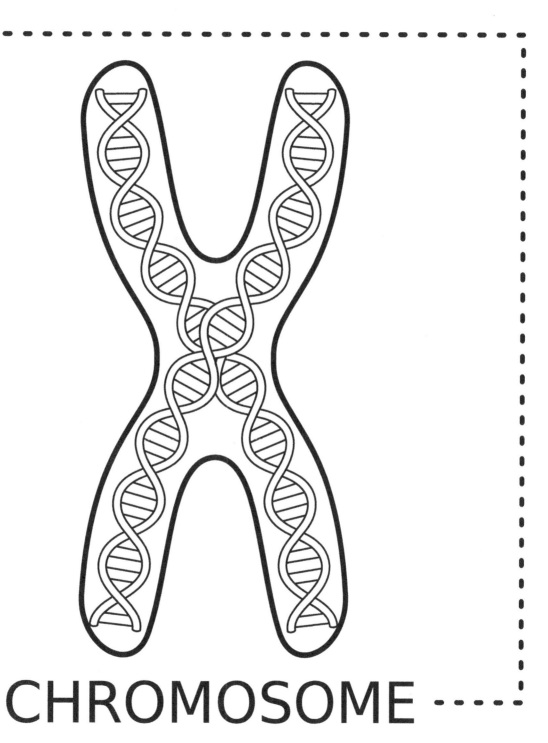

CHROMOSOME

Each image is printed single-sided to prevent bleed-through.

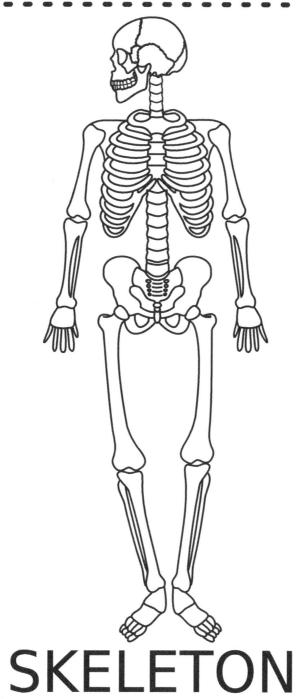

SKELETON

Each image is printed single-sided to prevent bleed-through.

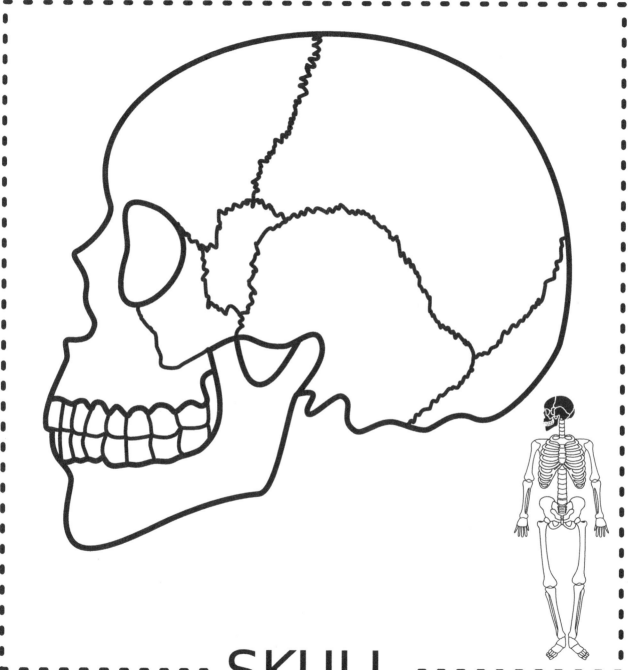

SKULL

Each image is printed single-sided to prevent bleed-through.

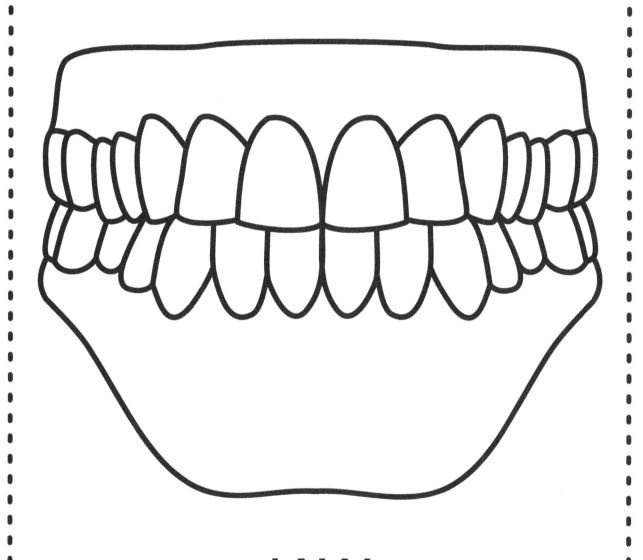

JAW

Each image is printed single-sided to prevent bleed-through.

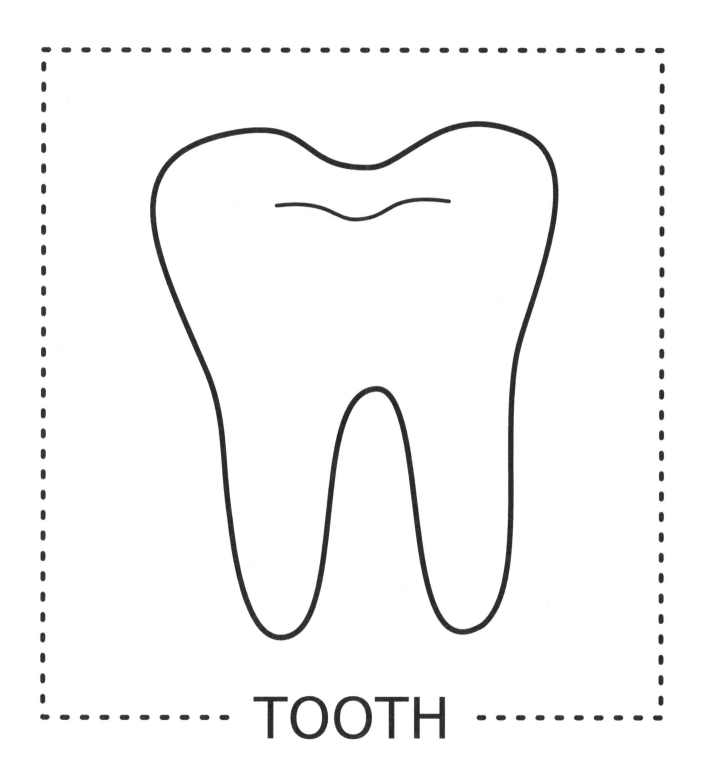

TOOTH

Each image is printed single-sided to prevent bleed-through.

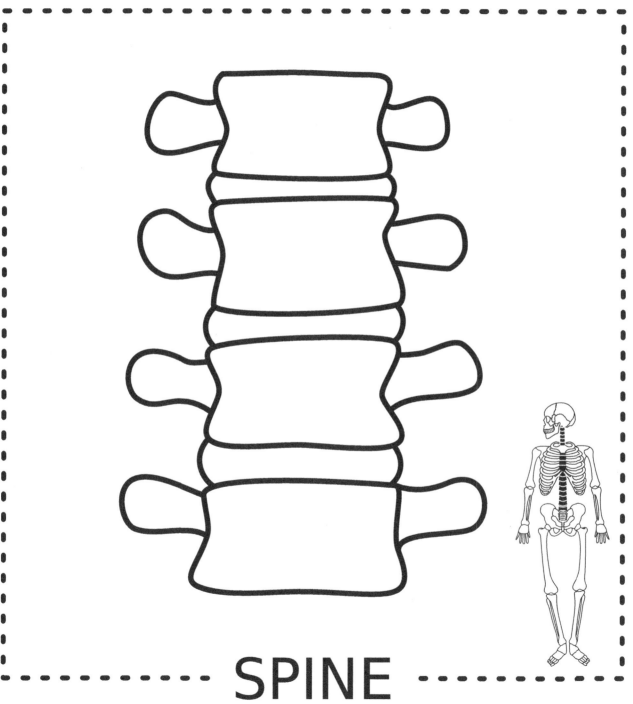

SPINE

Each image is printed single-sided to prevent bleed-through.

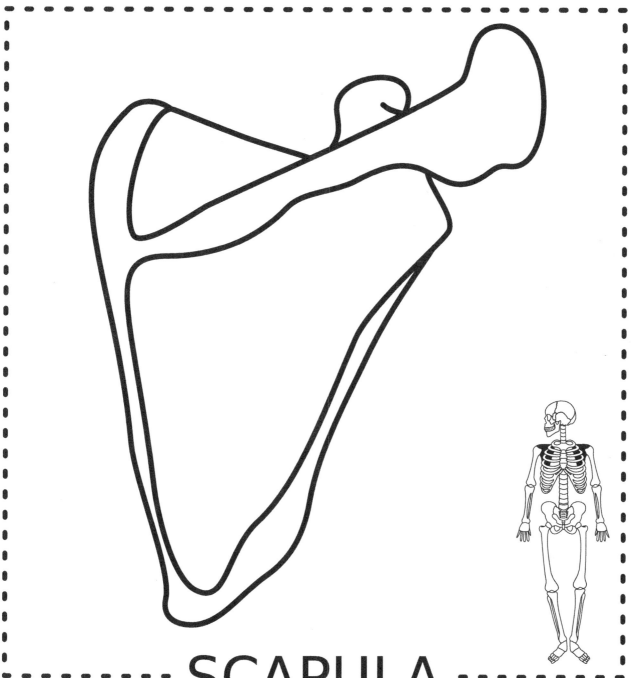

SCAPULA

Each image is printed single-sided to prevent bleed-through.

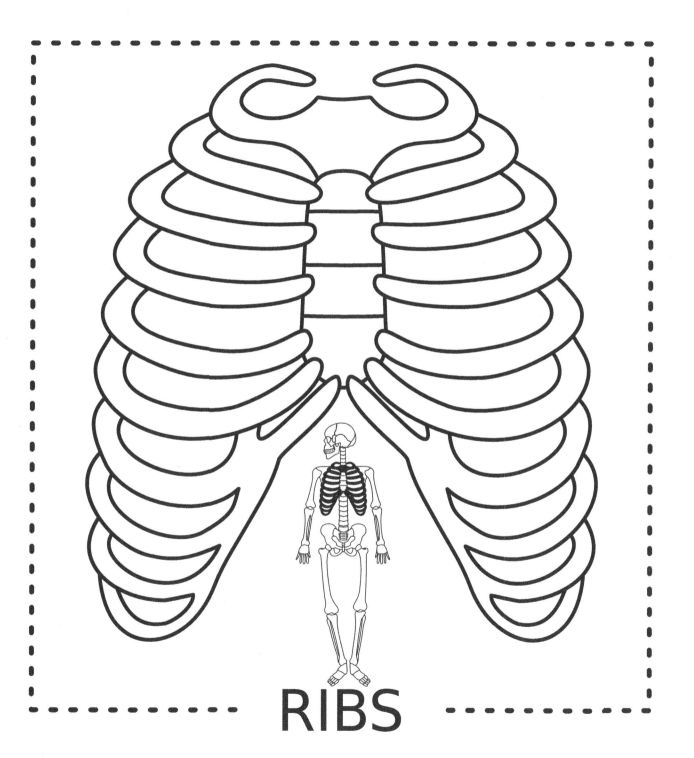

RIBS

Each image is printed single-sided to prevent bleed-through.

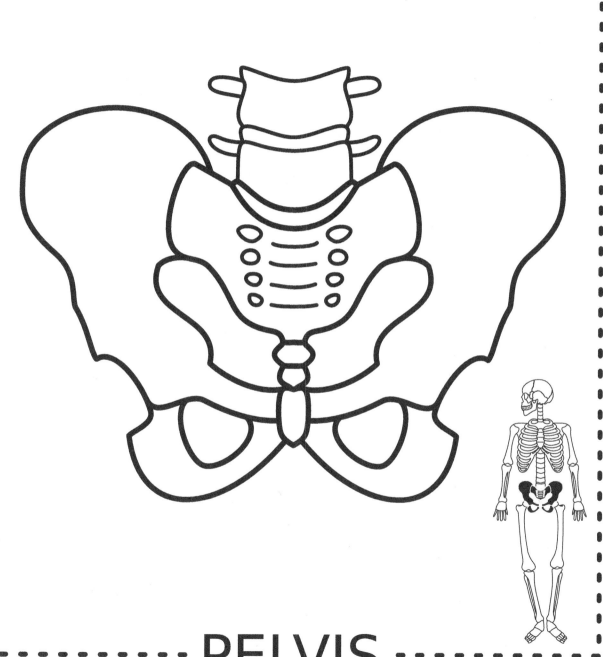

PELVIS

Each image is printed single-sided to prevent bleed-through.

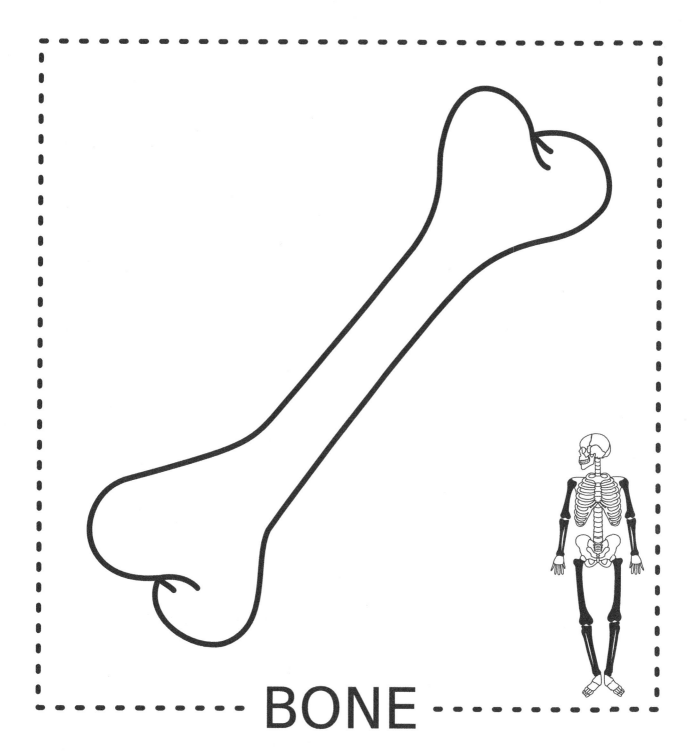

BONE

Each image is printed single-sided to prevent bleed-through.

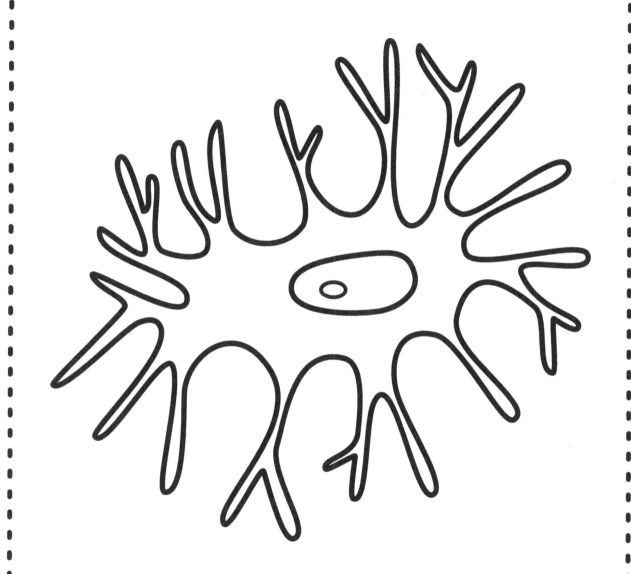

BONE CELL

Each image is printed single-sided to prevent bleed-through.

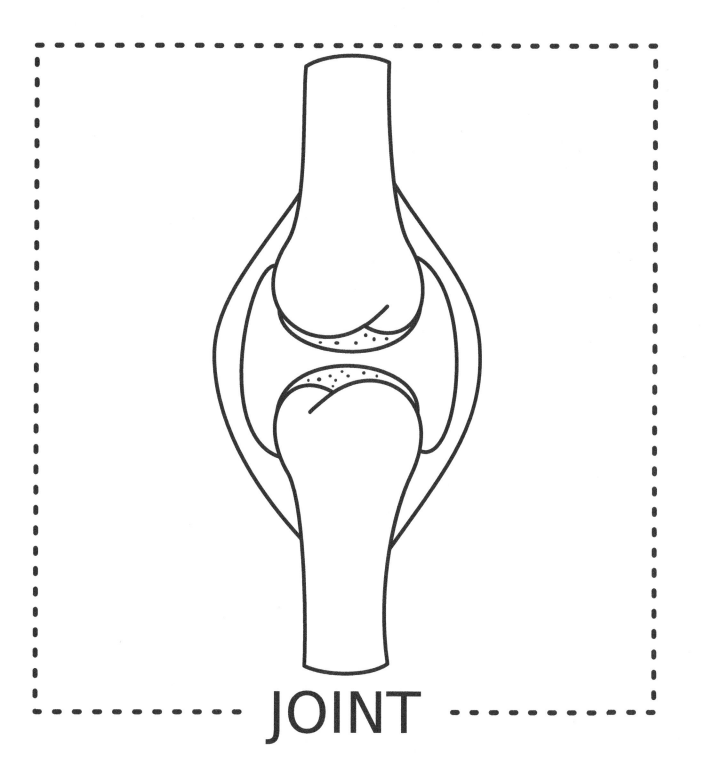

JOINT

Each image is printed single-sided to prevent bleed-through.

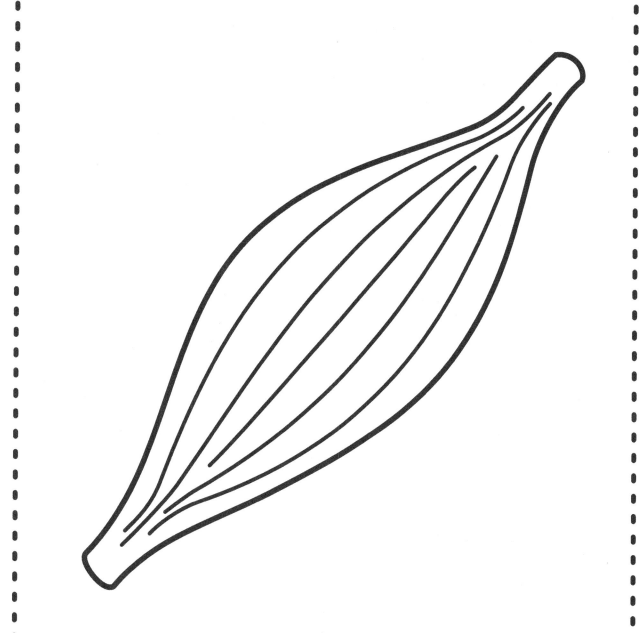

MUSCLE

Each image is printed single-sided to prevent bleed-through.

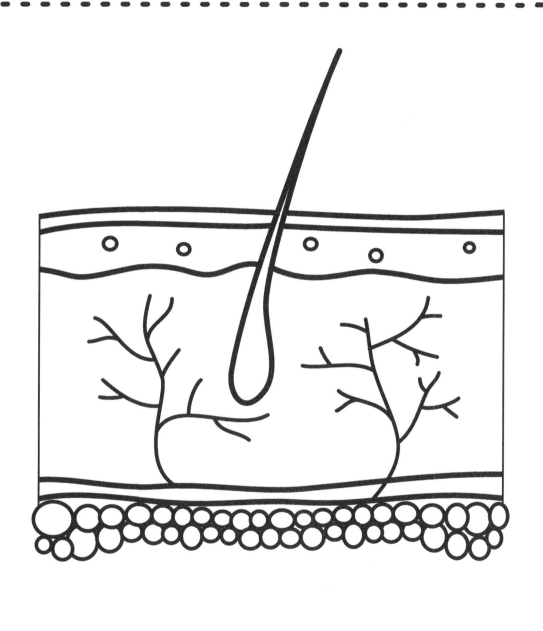

SKIN

Each image is printed single-sided to prevent bleed-through.

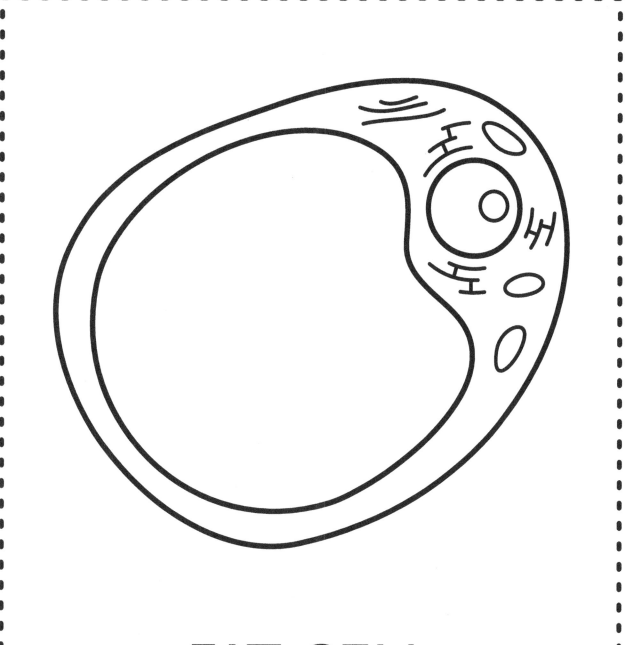

FAT CELL

Each image is printed single-sided to prevent bleed-through.

Made in the USA
Coppell, TX
10 December 2024

42214100R00059